WHY

NOT

ME?

ISBN 979-8-98507-930-2 (PRINT)

ISBN 979-8-98507-931-9 (EBOOK)

Contents

The Start 7

My Why... 17

A Little About Me... 27

Me and Kelly 37

Essential Oils 43

Learning How To... 53

Life... it Happens 61

Sometimes We Must Wait... 73

Changing Your Mindset.. 81

Small Changes You Can Make................................... 87

Reflecting on Life 95

About the Author... 103

Acknowledgments

God, thank you! Without you in my life, I would not have come as far as I have, I would not have the amazing family I have behind me and I would never have published this book!

Jessica Harris, your vision started me on this crazy insane journey of writing a book…. Never thought I would be publishing a book!!! Thank you!!!

Joe, my amazing husband!! You see in me some amazing talents that I never see, and you always help to bring them out. I never thought I would have the confidence to have been able to start businesses and write a book. Yet, here I am killing it, with you by my side pushing when I need, of course with an "I told ya so!" Thank you for being the rock of our family!! Love you so much I could never imagine life without you!!!!

Suzanne and Keegan you gave me the strength and courage to stand up to people. Something I never had done too much before I had you two. You have changed my life in so many wonderful ways, I could never thank you enough for picking me as your Mom. I will always be with you, besides you, in front of you or behind you, depending on where you need me to be!! You are amazing, caring, loving, respectful young adults and I am so very proud of the people you are becoming!! Never stop seeing the good in people and working hard for what you want!!!

To my amazing siblings, Kelly, Jonathan and Jessica! You are so very important to me and I can never express how much I love you guys!!! You are always there for me and I couldn't have come this far in life without you by my side!! I definitely got the best sisters and brother anyone could ever ask for!!! Thank you!!!!!!

For my amazing family who always is there for me!!! When things got crazy, all of you never faltered and always had my back. I could not have become the person I am today if you were not in my life!! I would not have the

5

life I have now if it weren't for all of you!!!! With all my

heart, I love you!!!!!

The Start

I was told I should write a book about things that happen in my life. I was also told by my friend, Jessica Harris, that she saw a vision of me at a book signing. She saw this vision while giving me a Reiki session. I got excited! Who was I going to see that was going to a book signing? So, I asked her whose book signing. I was told yours silly!!! Hahaha!! Really, me signing the books. I was told yes, it is your book you were signing…

Never did I think in a million years I would be writing a book. My life is crazy and normal at times. When it is crazy, it's a wild ride with a lot of high ups and low downs and all around the same time. When it is normal, it is normal. When it is crazy and upside down, it's a total mess.

So, I'm a daughter, grandchild, niece, sister, wife and mom. I am married to an amazing husband, who is my rock! I am blessed to have a daughter and a son. We have a dog, Roxie. I work and I am an entrepreneur too. So many hats, but I would not change any of them!

I have tried several times to start writing this book. And each time I started all over again because I did not know what I was supposed to write about or even how to go about it. Well, that all changed on a zoom call I was on. Of course, when I went to bed that night, I had no clue that at some strange hour of the night, that would all change. Of course, I have to start getting up when these things happen to me, but the issue is I need to get my sleep because like most everyone else in this world, I work a full time job, outside the home. But that night, it was different! The name of the book came to me and I remembered it! Then I was told that I was going to write about my life, but not in a "why me" way… It was a Why NOT Me way. This zoom called changed my life in so many ways and that is what I am going to write about. You will learn about things in my life, like we all go through, but my attitude was why me, of course that was always said when our lives are going "wrong". We never ask why me when things are going well. But what we should be asking is Why NOT Me?

So, if why NOT me, then why can't we also ask why NOT you?

I have learned recently that a lot has to do with mindset. Mine was in the negative mindset. Little do we realize that from an early age, we are told that we cannot do things. Yup, I am guilty of doing that to myself and my kids. Even to my husband too. It does not mean I do not support them; it means I would think, go ahead, and try, it most likely will not work. Well, if it did work, it was amazing. But if it did not work, we did not think outside the box and fail forward! We did not pick ourselves up and think of another way to try to work for something we wanted. We just failed and stayed where we were, we did not move on, just dwelled in the failure.

So, mindset is not easy to change, I can personally tell you that. So, here is an example. I am away on vacation for a few days, 5 day get away with my family. My husband likes to race, so we are in PA at Maple Grove Raceway. We stay at a hotel (about 20 minutes) from the racetrack. We have a dog about a year now, her name is Roxie. We leave Thursday morning, early, 4am. Ok, so I am usually nervous about doing things. We have this conversion van (it seats 9 people) so it is a big van. Then we haul this 29-foot trailer behind us. And NO, I am NOT driving!!!! I am hoping that I NEVER have to drive those two things together! I usually think OMG what ifs.... Well, mindset, I start by changing my what ifs (the bad) into what if you have a great time!! What if... while we are driving. Nope, the roads will not be congested because we left early, and we will be able to drive right through. Ok, not driving through is not an option. Two kids and a dog!!! Ya know we are going to be stopping for pee breaks and food. Better to stop for that then to be stuck in traffic.

Now before we left on Thursday morning, my husband tells me he checked the weather for where we are going. Rain on Friday and possibly the weekend. So, I ask, do we go? UM, yes, my husband says, we need to get away. Especially with all that was happening in the world, COVID. Then I find out the other wives that go decided not to come because of the rain or their husbands are not coming because they are not racing. Which leaves me, with my daughter, son, and a dog with all these racing men…. UM!!! I asked should I go to my husband. LOL, he says yes!!! OK, to me, God is saying you need to get away and go. So, we go, and I am the only wife there. But I can hang with the best of them!!! So, Thursday was crazy hot, got the trailer set up and the dog stressed most of the time, which makes me worry. She did not eat all day but she had some water. At least the guys that came up Thursday were also dog lovers and they all hung with her. Mind you, others were supposed to come up on Friday, but the rain kept them away, they'll be coming up Saturday morning to race and no, no more women coming up.

Since it was raining Friday, I decided to stay back in the hotel with the dog; my husband and kids went to the track to meet up with the guys that stayed in the trailer at the track. Oh, they are having a great time riding bikes and golf carts in the rain. That would be my kids, I am sure the bigger kids will be joining soon too! Anyway, my whole point of this story now that you have the background is, mindset. The old mindset me would have bitched and complained about being "stuck" in the hotel with the dog. But since my mindset changed, I had the time and quietness to start my writing my book.

While in the hotel, the fire alarm goes off, and I am writing my book. OMG neither me nor the dog were expecting that, but who ever does? I have lived through a house fire, just 6 months after my husband and I were married. So, I totally get a little bit crazy and into full blown "get out" mode when this happens. Roxie was in the corner of the room not knowing what is going on. I am trying to get my shoe on so I can get us out (of course into the rain) but I am in a boot for my left foot. All this fun!! While trying to get my boot on, I started laughing to myself. Yes, laughing.

The fire alarm in my room finally went off, I checked the hallway no smoke. I call the front desk, asking if we need to vacate the hotel. He said not to, as he was having maintenance check into why the alarms were going off. He said something about cleaning chemicals that were mixed and should not have been that made smoke. I texted my husband, starting off with "you cannot make this shit up", and told him what happened. When he finally read the text, he asked if we were outside. LOL I would be calling him every second until he answered to come get us, it is raining!! The "old" me would have let this ruin my day. Stop writing my book, been in panic, upset mode the rest of the day. But mindset changes things and how you look and deal with things. I got the dog settled right next to me on the couch, almost in my lap. I had put everything down and let Roxie get settled with me petting her to stop her from shaking. The fire alarms went off a few times more but for short times. They made sure to turn the alarms in the rooms off almost right away while the hallway ones took a minute or two longer. Now that things have quieted down, I stopped and gave thanks to God. Yes, the "old" me would never have done that either. I gave thanks for the fire alarms and for everything I do have. Yes, you read that right. Thanks for the fire alarms that went off. Should there have been a real fire and they did not go off, there would have been a bigger problem in the hotel. Thanks also for my abilities, the things that happened Thursday. A few of my customers texted me what they need or to get together. For being able to be calm during the fire alarm and not having to go outside in the rain!!! LOL Yes, I did give thanks for that. I have also thanked God for learning how to change my mindset and notice and stop the negative when I need to.

So, I am now back on track, Roxie next to me sleeping, essential oils on me, computer on my lap and my phone by my side to do some research for a friend who needs essential oils when I get back from my vacation. I can't believe how much I have changed, and I am excited to tell you all about it. The hard and the easy, the "I don't believe that" and how I have changed that too.

Please know, I will speak about God, I am not forcing you or telling you that you need to believe in God. Whatever your belief system is, that is where you need to "insert" when I talk about God. That is MY belief. I do feel everyone has to believe in something. If you do not, find out what it is you believe in. Look around, lots of beautiful things, but really look. This world can be mean, and it's polluted, and it can be very discouraging. How can all of nature survive in this world? To me, there is something better out there, to me it is God. Do not just go with whatever anyone tells you, you must decide for yourself. I used to hear; we are killing the earth and I used to believe it. I listen to a wise person I know, Jihan Solomon Thomas. She states that the earth will always win. Ya know, she is a million percent correct. I look at places that have been destroyed, blown up and devastated by so many different things. Then you look at pictures of places that have no people of inhabitance and look at how green the foliage is, buildings covered in whatever is growing there. Now it might not be inhabitable for people, but the earth is flourishing and looking so beautiful. We might be trying to kill earth, but when we are all gone from the earth, the earth will heal itself and take care of itself and the animals in it.

Ah, the animals. They rely on God to give them everything they need, food, shelter, and all. We as humans do not rely on God. We used to, but we have decided that we can do it better and we no longer have the faith, if you will, in God to know that he will provide for us.

Ok, I know this is the book I am supposed to write, I have gotten farther than any other I time I have started with interruptions!! Especially fire alarms and a scared dog! It is taken on a life of its own and I know I am on the right track this time. I really hope you continue to read and come to my book signing!

My Why

Ok, so how did I get started on this journey? It started a little over 5 years ago because of my son. By this time in my life I started to pray a lot to God. I knew God was always there, but never relied on Him for help. Different things for different reasons, but I had to go back to God. I lost my way at one point in my life. I was upset and mad at Him. I asked why me a lot, the problem is it was not the correct question. I should have been asking why NOT me. But at the time, I had lost my faith and was so desperate and willing to try ANYTHING.

But all I saw was the negative in my life at that point in time. Maybe we should start with a little background. Life was never easy for me. I was not well liked in school at all. My mom got divorced when I was three and my sister was just born. She moved back in with her parents and my aunts and uncles. It was tight quarters where we were. My mom is one of 6 children. My mom was not the nicest person. Everyone was out to get her, that was her mindset, and she gave me that mindset early on. Once you are given a certain mindset from your parent(s) it's hard to get rid of, especially since your parents are the ones to always have your back and are supposed to be your biggest cheering section, right? Well, not all parents are that way. My Mom was not one of them. She poisoned me against my father, her own parents, sisters, and brothers. But I and my sister were too young at that time to realize it. We realized it later in life and she had done some serious damage with relationships we did not even know how to even start to repair them. Unfortunately, my sister and I, lost some people before we could repair those relationships, my father being one of them. Some of the things we learned along the way! We no longer have our mom in our life, we made that tough decision together. We have a family that is amazing, and we could not have asked for a better family. Do not get me wrong, we have our fights and our disagreements, just like any other family, but when push came to shove, our family always had our backs! The family I am talking about is my mom's parents (both gone now), her brothers and sister (their spouses and kids), my step mom and my other brother and sister (my dad's kids with his wife). UM, PLEASE do not say, that is your half blah blah blah!!!! NO, THEY ARE MY BROTHER AND SISTER!! I feel like that with anyone who has a "half" brother or sister.

Ok, my son, Keegan, was always sick. Colds and once a year we had something that really took him down, flu, bronchitis, and the last straw for this momma, was pneumonia. UGH, the sleepless week because this kid would be coughing his head off all night long. Mommy and Keegan were cranky!!! Long before this time, I started thinking that there had to be a better way to help Keegan with his immune system. But I did not know what to do or where to go. So, I prayed, and I prayed every chance I got. A lot of crying and feeling like I was horrible Mom. Let us face it, most of us have been there, feeling helpless and desperate to try ANYTHING. At first, it was to find something to help Keegan. I had no idea what I needed for Keegan, but I needed something, and I at least knew that. That was the start, knowing I needed something. So, I prayed for help to find what I needed. So, by now, I am at my wits end and I am so desperate and will try literally anything!!!!

So, God answered my prayers, but I will tell you when you pray, you must LISTEN and you must OBEY. Yes, it feels weird to type those words and even harder to do them! Also, please know you will get your answer ANYWHERE and/or ANYTIME. I got my answer scrolling through Facebook. I kept seeing an event on a group I am in. I kept dismissing the event because we teach our children not to go to strangers' houses. Well, every time I prayed the image of this event came into my mind. Then I looked for the event, which took me time, because of course when you are looking for something, you cannot find it easily. So, I finally found it and read the information on it again. All I could think of is how on earth is this stuff going to help Keegan? No possible way!!! I disregarded the event again and kept going. Of course, I'm still praying and when I'm on Facebook and thinking what am I going to do to help my son and stop failing him, of course this event pops up almost every other scroll on Facebook. Ok, I finally gave in. I am going to go there, but of course, I told my husband where I was going, told him I needed to check this out. He said who is this? I said a stranger's house. LOL call me in an hour and make sure I am ok. If not call the police. Of course, we laughed then he asked if I was serious. I said yes. I do not know this woman and I must go. He told me I was crazy and wanted to know what I was going to buy. I said nothing because this stuff will never work, but I must go because God is telling me to go. I explained what was happening when I was praying. He told me he thinks I might be losing my mind and going crazy. Yup, I agreed, at that time. Little did we know that we would laugh at this story and it was the 1st step of our lives starting to be changed for the better. So,

I went and spoke to this women, listened to what she was talking about, how it changed her families lives and she had some friends there to support her and I got to speak to them and pick their brains too.

Well, I did buy something. That was step number two. Then I had to come home and tell my husband. He was not happy with what I purchased and told me it will not work. I told him I think he is correct, but after praying and this keeps coming up, I had to go and my gut told me purchase it! Dive right in!!!! I never really realized it until now how these small steps started my new life. I had not known it yet at all, I was still in the mind set "why me"? By the time my kit had come in, I called the person who helped me with my purchase. I told her what do I do now? I am in a brain fog; no sleep doesn't make the mind work well and being worried about my son added to that.

Margaret, the person who helped me with the kit and helped me learn why it would help, came right over. She never hesitated to help me, even with a child with pneumonia. She told me which essential oils would help support my son's respiratory and immune systems. I tried everything she told me. I got my kit late afternoon. Keegan slept that night I started using the essential oils on him. I figured it was a fluke, but I kept using the oils the next day all day, just as Margaret showed me. That next night, Keegan and I both slept like rocks!!! Not one cough that had us both up all night. WHAT??? Yes, I was so happy I got to sleep that night. I kept up with what Margaret told me and Keegan had a follow up in a few days. OK, we will see what the doctor says. Because ya know, he is a doctor and knows better than I, right? I later learned that answer was a "no" quite often; I felt comfortable, at that point in time, just blindly doing what the doctors said and give the children, but I was "just the mom". His doctor said that his lungs sounded great and he was a little shocked that it was clearing up so well and fast. He asked what I did; I said essential oils. He laughed at me. I was upset and it really put me off with my kids' doctor's office. I now do not feel comfortable doing what the doctor's tell me without asking a million questions. I am the mother and my gut knows better.

Another thing I will tell you LISTEN TO YOUR GUT FEELINGS!! Yes, they can take you places you might not want to go, however, it is God talking to you. Your gut feeling is your intuition. It is usually right all the time, if not I will say 99% of the time.

Here is an example of mine and my sister's gut feelings working. Kelly, my sister, and I have a gut feeling that is usually connected. About 25 years ago, we were going out with friend's midnight bowling. It was so much fun, and we had such a great time. My boyfriend (husband now) was driving. He put on his seatbelt, which he usually did not do. Kelly and I looked at each other. There were a total of 5 in the car and a few others were meeting us there. When Kelly and I looked at each other, one of her friends saw our look at each other. She was so scared. She said she's seen that look on Kelly when her intuition was going and this time, she saw the look on my face too. She made everyone put on their seatbelts, even if they were in the back seat. I think she said a prayer before we started driving.

Well, our gut feelings were right. While driving on the Southern State Parkway some idiot was in the left-hand lane and decided that he wanted to get off on the exit that was coming up. The problem was that he cut across all lanes to make the exit, which he almost missed. He also almost hit us, thank God Joe had some quick reaction time to avoid the accident. Kelly and I looked at each other and we both knew it was not over. This guy was finally away from us, he took off driving like a crazy person. But of course, he hit some traffic and we caught up to him. This time, we were in the left-hand turning lane and this idiot was in the right lane. Well, he decided, again last minute, he needed to a make a left-hand turn. He pulled the same stunt he did on the parkway. Again, thanks to Joe seeing this idiot start to move towards us and his quick reaction time, we were able to avoid this jerk from hitting us again. We did see cops sitting in a parking lot. Joe drove over to them and explained what happened and the cops could see that we were all a little shaken up about what happened. The cops said there was nothing they could do; they did not see it. Again, gut feeling and intuition. Listen to it. This was to let us know something was about to happen. You never know what is going to happen, but it is a warning to stay on your toes.

As time went on, I stopped listening to my gut feelings. When I had kids, it came back and this time stronger than I could ever imagine. All this time, I felt like something was missing. Not sure what, but something. I had to stop being a blinded sheep.

A Little About Me

So as stated earlier, my parents got divorced when I was about 3 and my sister, Kelly, was just born. We moved with our mom into her parents' full house. We made it work. My mom was a little crazy then, but the "normal" was my mom getting upset because everyone was against her and no one loved or cared about her. When I got older, elementary school age, who in the world would think that their mom was crazy? Thinking my dad did not want to see us (more like being told my dad did not want to see us) and giving us the "impression" that she loved us.

I was not liked by my school peers. Really, no one liked me. I had a friend or two, but it was not any lasting friendship. Throughout elementary school, I really did not have any friends. I had one friend from the neighborhood. She was nice to me and never made me feel like she did not like me. So, she was really my only friend. School was hard for me with no friends. I was always made fun of. Children can be very mean.

When your mom drills into you how much the family does not like her or you, it starts to get to you and you start believing it. It is hard to believe the one person who is supposed to be in your corner and on your side is lying to you. So that was the start of where I got to where I was. The strange thing is that when I was around my family, they never made me feel like I was not loved by them, as my mom always told me. I always felt strange, like I was out of place at times, like the black sheep. But for some reason I knew they loved me.

My mom finally got enough money to get a place of our own. Right down the block from her parents and it was great! We could still see the rest of the family and have our own place. Then my mom got remarried to an asshole. He was abusive to me in several ways. It was a terrible time for me. I watched a show with my mom, "Something About Amelia". Strange I can still remember the name of the TV show. After seeing that show I told a friend at school that I was Amelia. I asked her not to tell anyone. Well, that was my huge cry for help! That did not go well at first. The police showed up at school and I was even more terrified to go home. I did not want him to kill me or my family. I was in middle school when I told, figured I know better that I would be safe and so will my family, but being terrified out of your mind does horrible things to you. The second time the police came to the school I told them everything. It was even more of a nightmare than I could ever have imagined! My mom was called down to the police station. Then leaving us at the police station and taking her husband home at 3AM. She told the police to call her parents, and they would pick me and my sister up. Thank God they did. I did not have any doubt in my mind they would come for us. They came running!!!

My grandparents were foster parents before this for many years and had numerous kids. One of their last foster kids was adopted by them. Back then, you were not allowed to adopt your foster child(ren). They were one of the few people to help get this law changed. So, when I decided to stay with my grandparents, they had been re-instated as foster parents. I was happy, I would not have stayed in any other house. The judge told my mom to have her husband move out if she wanted to have me and/or my sister move back in. Kelly wanted to move back with mom because she felt she did not want to leave mom alone. She felt no one in the family, including me, loved her. That was because that is what my mom told her.

Now I was older and understood a little bit more about my mom, but Kelly was younger and did not, in my eyes. So, mom's husband moved out and Kelly moved back in and I stayed with my grandparents.

For about a month, I had to meet my mom once a weekend for lunch. Lunch was her driving around asking me who I had sex with at school. I got called a lot of horrible names by her. Then she would drop me off at my grandparents' house. She chose to not go in because she stopped talking to her family. The family tried to help my mom.

My family asked her why she took her second husband home. He was an adult and you should never leave your children. Well, she was incapable of caring for us the way a parent should care for their children, in my opinion. She stopped talking to them. She was offered help by everyone in my family. Many years later, I was told that my one Uncle had offered her money for a divorce from her second husband; an apartment for the three of us (my mom, me and Kelly) and therapy for all of us. He wanted to help us and get us the best help he could. She turned him down, because I was a lying bitch (along with many other horrible names) and she stayed with her husband. To say I thanked God every day for my family is an understatement. It just goes to show you how wrong my mom was about her family. She obviously has some mental problems, in my opinion.

She would go back to my sister and tell her I was coming home next weekend. Which was a lie. It also made my sister not talk to me anymore when we did see each other. My mom would bring Kelly over to my grandparents' house to see the family, and Kelly stopped talking to me all together. It was obvious Kelly was upset with me, but when I asked why, she would not tell me. Well, my aunts and uncles were visiting and put me and Kelly in the kitchen and stayed at the doorways until we talked. Kelly said how much she had hated me because I left her alone with mom and that I lied about coming home. I asked who told you I was moving back with mom? She said mom. YUP, my mom was a master at manipulation. She did a number on mine and my sister's relationship. Took us a few years and a lot of work to get back what we had and got stronger during that time. If it were not for my aunts and uncles, Kelly and I would have never had that talk that day and who knows where we would be today in our relationship. But since our family cared, they made sure that hard talk happened and I am glad it did. It brought us closer together. It also made us both realize how sick our mother was.

I had to testify against her husband in family court. He plea bargained for criminal court to spare the families of another hearing. How nice of him! Testifying was scary. He had a lawyer that was yelling at the judge and the court guards did not like that too much!! The one guard told me "when I tell you, get down and do not move until I come get you!" While he is telling me this, the lawyer is yelling at the Judge and trying to get closer to him and the court officer getting ready to pull his gun because this lawyer was not listening. I went white as a ghost!!! I could not stop shaking with the lawyer fighting and yelling at the Judge. He finally stopped when he realized the court officers were not liking that at all and reaching for their guns!!!!! The judge took a small break for me after that. One of the hardest things was to testify about the abuse that occurred. It was even harder to testify since one of the court officers in the room was someone I knew.

During my second day of testifying, my grandfather had a major heart attack. I got out of testifying to find out I had to go to the hospital later that night. They did not expect my grandfather to make it. I so did not want to go to the hospital!! I did go because I had to and was made to. But it was with shots of sambuca and a beer in me!! Yes, I was underage, and I was under the supervision of my uncle and aunt. I did nothing but cry!!! They say what does not kill you makes you stronger right? Well, I was being crushed by the biggest boulder you could find, and I could not breathe at all. But I lived with the grace and strength of God. I did everything "on my own" and did not give it to God! HUGE MISTAKE, but I did not know that then. I knew something was out there that was bigger than me and I knew God was out there too, but I did not realize He was IT! I did not realize I could give it all to God and not take it back!

I never spoke about the details of my abuse or what happened to me. There was only one person who had asked me questions about my abuse, and I answered, but not 100%

honest. I left out details. I could see in this person's eyes, that I was killing them by telling them what I did tell, I never wanted to put anyone through that. So, I told myself, I would never tell what happened to me in detail to anyone, I could not let that kill them the way it killed me. My relationship with this person has never been the same since. I am totally heartbroken over it!

My grandfather pulled through, however, he had to have major heart surgery. They opened him up to find three different types of cancer in him. I started to know God as time went on from there. My grandfather did pass in August, after I graduated high school. It was 6 days after my birthday. Again, hard times and I still did not know enough to give it to God.

My relationship with my father was a little bit better, but not much. I had to stop listening to the voice of my mom in my head of how much he never wanted to be with us. Truth be told, she stopped him a lot of times from coming to see us. It is hard to get that voice out of your head when it has been in there for so long. It is like deep trenches that you must climb to get out of and make new trenches without falling into the old ones.

My sister finally moved in with my grandmother and me. That was because she was eighteen and mom's husband could move back into the house. He was mean about things and she moved out! As I said he is a jerk (and that is putting it nicely). It was nice to have my sister back with me. I really did miss her so much! From here is when my life started to feel a little "normal".

Me and Kelly

So, Kelly moves in with me and Nan. YAY!! So happy I got my sister back and away from our mom and her husband. So, life goes on, dating and such. Sister fights and quarrels. I still must learn how to look myself in the mirror with all my scars. I fight myself all the time. How do I stop saying "it's my fault"? Yes I went to therapy, but it's still not always easy.

Well, to be honest, we have very little contact with mom. We would prefer not to have any, but Nan feels that she is still our mother and we should keep in contact with her. So, to keep Nan happy, we have a little contact with her. She is still married to her perfect husband and still thinks that we are wrong for leaving her. She obviously forgot she left us at the police station.

I met Joe, eventually he and I would be married. Joe got an apartment and I eventually moved in with him. We got engaged and it was awesome. Joe proposed when my whole family was home for Christmas. He knows how important my family is to me. When we got engaged, his mom kept bothering him to find out when she was going to meet my mom. UGH, it really got them into some heated talks. I had a lunch with my future mother-in-law. I explained we (Kelly and I) do not speak very often to mom and we have very little contact with her due to the abuse her second husband inflicted on me. Joe did not tell his mom about my past, knowing how I felt about it. He also felt it was up to me to tell anyone I wanted and not him.

She was understanding but there were a lot of questions. I answered as best as I could, as I felt I really did not want anyone in his family to know that at that time. They did not know me well enough.

Well, it turns out when mom hears I got engaged, she called me and Kelly to have lunch with her. She had told us that she moved out of her apartment with her husband and is leaving him. That lead us to believe that she was divorcing him. That is what you do when you leave your husband, right? Mom asked if she could be a part of our lives again. Kelly and I said we had to think about it. By now, Kelly is dating Jerry (who will be her husband). We asked Joe and Jerry about this. We were not sure if we wanted to give her a second chance, and we needed opinions from people we could trust and were outsiders. Both Jerry and Joe said that they would stand behind us and that the decision was ours to make. It was a hard decision and we really did not know what to do. Do we give her another chance? She technically had a chance at the police station, and she choose her husband, not her children. That is not the decision of a normal person who "loves" her children. We thought and talked a lot. We never wanted to say "what if" if we did not give her another chance. This time we thought it was different, she left the apartment and got a place of her own and she did say she was leaving him. Well, we gave her another chance. We decided that if one of us says no, the answer is no for the both of us. We had to both agree about this decision and if something happens and one stops talking with her, we both did. So, we agreed to give her another chance. She is our mom, right? Maybe things will be different. Please remember a tiger never changes their stripes. We explained to our family that we started talking to her again and they all gave us their opinions that they did not think it was a great idea. They would stand behind us, but they did not feel it was the best thing. A real family (and true and real friends) are the ones that can tell you how they feel but will still stand behind you. And when things fall apart, they are there to help you and pick you up. Which they did. Mom never really did "leave" her husband. They enjoyed dinners during the week, going away on vacations and speaking to him every day and night.

Kelly and I tried to work through it, but the feeling of this not being right never went away. But things got worse when I had my first child. Mom was at my house once a week to help with babysitting when I went back to work. Things did not work out as time went on. Kelly and I had a long talk one day, she was pregnant, and things were not feeling right for a long time and Kelly and I noticed that things between us were not right. Not in a bad horrible way, but just not good between us. We spoke for a while and decided that she had to go for good.

We spoke to Joe and Jerry and told them we were going to stop talking to mom and never let her back into our lives again! For good too!! Of course, Joe and Jerry were both behind us and our decision. They understood what was going on and how it had affected us, as they were living with us and it affected them having her in their lives. Next, we told our family, they also were behind us, worried about us and of course there for us. Real family, nothing like mom told us, and they were there for anything we needed, a hug and talking when needed. Never an "I told you so" or "you're on your own".

One of my uncles once told me that they (the family) knew something was "wrong" with me, but they could never put their finger on it. They felt horrible that I suffered for so long before I told, and they could not figure out what was wrong with me. But once I told them, they all understood, the missing puzzle pieces. Finally, a lot of things I did or did not do made sense to them. I kind of felt relief when he told me that. I meant they really cared enough about me and obviously spoke to each other and tried to figure out what was going on. Which means that mom was totally wrong about our family!! They did care and they showed us that they never left us either!

That changed my mind about our family. They basically had the door shut on them by mom, but they never did anything to make me and Kelly feel that they were going to treat us the way mom treated them.

Essential Oils

Remember, I prayed for help with my 25son. I was on a mission to help him not get sick so much and I was willing to try anything!!!! At least once a year he was sick with something horrible like the flu, bronchitis, and pneumonia. Not to mention the usual colds when that time of year comes around. Every year it was a stronger antibiotic every time, he was only seven or eight years old when he had pneumonia. Being desperate and at the end of your rope, you will try anything. I mean anything!!!! My feelings were that there was something out there that could help him and all of us, but I had no clue what. Just my gut feeling telling me that there was something out there and I had to find it. I had no clue what I was looking for. So what did I do? I prayed to God!!! This is when you need to listen and obey when you get your answers from God. This is one of the hardest parts, being obedient!!!! Not easy at all. It

took me a few weeks to listen and go to Margaret's house!!
I obviously finally went. It was the best thing I ever did, and
I never looked back.

So, now I must tell my husband that I am going to a
stranger's house to listen to her talk about something I do
not think will help Keegan. He laughed at me. I had one
request, do not tell the kids that I am going to a stranger's
house. We teach our kids not to talk to strangers and go with
them, but here I am going to a house I have no clue who the
person is. YUP I did not want to get grief from my kids. I
gave my husband the address and told him if he did not hear
from me in about an hour, to call the cops. About an hour
and a half, because I lost track of time, my husband calls
me. I can hear in his voice that he is hoping I answered the
phone. Thank God I did answer it! He said it is over an hour
and I did not hear from you, where are you? I said I am
good and was just finishing up with Margaret. I would be
home soon, so he said you are OK, I said yes. See you soon.

He was happy I was home and now Margaret is a great friend!

Margaret was great with making me feel comfortable and took the time to really talk to me and answer all of my questions. I am so grateful for her time and patience. She has become such a great friend to me. Another reason I am glad I got involved with this company and community, the people I have met along the way have become my famOILY (ha-ha pun intended). They are my community and love me for how I think because we think alike. So, unlike what I told my husband, I am not buying anything, it is not going to work. I also hope that I can be that person to help someone like Margaret has done for me. Remember, I was desperate!!! My son was suffering and I had no idea what to do. The doctors could not give me any answers and had no clue on what could boost his immune system, as they told me it was fine… UM NO, it was not. I was getting done with what people were telling me and my gut was screaming at me. I am done with ignoring my screaming gut feelings!!

I used to always rely on them, and they never let me down.

Well, time to get back to listening to them. The more I

listened to my gut, the more I felt like a black sheep. Which

is why I stopped listening. But that was the wrong decision.

Now I am back to the right decision! I will embrace being a

black sheep!!!!

So, essential oils. I did not know much about them

but I learned that they are the plants' immune system.

Interesting, right? Look at all the pollutants in the air today.

Now, go look at your favorite plant, flower, bush, or tree.

How does it look when it is blooming? Beautiful?

Awesome! Now think about all the pollutants in the air.

INTERESTING!!! Mind blown or no? God made them, so

of course they would be beautiful. OK, so if we think about

it, which I never did until I listened to Jihan Thomas talk or

even better, listen to one of her rants!!! They are

AMAZING! She is amazing by the way. Look her up and

listen to her.

So, she talks about how medicine is made in the labs. Honestly, I never thought about it. Doctors give us medicine to help us, but it is made in a lab. How did they know what to make? Well, scientists look at the makeup of the immune systems of the plants. They see something in the makeup of the immune system in the plant that works well for your – pick something – and they take that "item" from the makeup of the plant and make it in a lab. The issue I see, it is like taking a piece of someone's DNA because that is the best of it. Well, the whole thing is what makes it "work" not the "best" strand of the DNA. Not sure I am explaining it correctly.

So, you take medicine for something, your thyroid which is part of your endocrine system. The lab makes medicine that will help your endocrine system work better. The doctors say it will help your thyroid that you have been having problems with. But it is only a piece of the strand that the scientists were looking at, not the whole string of DNA. Well, first, it is made in a lab which means it is synthetic not natural or from God and nature. So, you take this medicine the doctors give you. Now after taking this medication, you find out what the side effects are and that it does damage to another organ. Now the doctor will put you on another medication to help with that issue. Let us hope that the medications can work together and not have any bad reactions using both of those medications together. Again, another synthetic medication. Again, I listened to Jihan talk about this. It was an eye opener for me. So, my question is this, the essential oils I use, that come from the plants' immune system, can they be considered natural or natures medicine? Jihan also speaks about eating better, more vegetables and fruits. Also, movement, you need to have some sort of exercise. And mindset!!!!!! BOMB!!!!!!! My mind is totally blown!!!!!! Just listen to her and you will totally understand!

Yes, you can use an essential oil to help your endocrine system work better. The best part of this, which I totally LOVE, is that whatever you take will not harm other systems in your body!! Yes, please read that again!! OK I am going off on a tangent and I think maybe that should be another book?? But all of this made sense to me. So, I am so happy I am with this community.

This does not mean that we do not need modern medicine. But, if we can use a holistic and natural remedies to boost our bodies systems so that they work better and together, then maybe we do not need modern medicine all the time. I think of my son who needed stronger antibiotics every time he was sick because his body build up an immunity to the strength he was given. We do need them, but the less sometimes the better.

What I learned about essential oils, is that they help support your body's systems and the oils can help more than one organ. The beauty of this, if the organ does not need anything from that essential oil, it just passes through. Nothing gets "hurt" or "harmed" from using the oils. Your body just lets it move through and goes to another system or it leaves your body. Now, let me ask you a question, does the medication from the pharmacy do that? Does it not "hurt" or "harm" any organs or systems? You can answer this question and decide for yourself. I never knew that about a pure therapeutic grade essential oils when I started with them. Nor did I know when I started, that there are different grades of essential oil. There is a lot I have learned on my journey with the oils. During this book I will tell you more and you can always reach out to me to ask your questions.

So, did you find Jihan Solmon Thomas? Did you listen to her? Are you interested in getting some oils? Well, here is one of my links, www.getoiling.com/ellenscaccio click here or type that in and you can contact me and sign up.

So, I get my essential oils and call Margaret. My kit came in the afternoon, and I was so tired from not sleeping that week. When an 8-year-old with pneumonia is not sleeping at night because he is up coughing all night, Mom does not sleep either! Margaret comes over knowing my son is sick and helps me. She helps me get set up with the diffuser, which oils to support his systems and gives me a huge hug and tells me, call me when you need to. Even if you forget, she obviously knew I was a zombie and going to forget, call me. Thankfully, I did not forget what she told me to do, I was smart and wrote it down the second she left!

So, I did what Margaret told me to do. Joe, my husband, looked at me and said I was nuts and I agreed with him.

Ya know, we are told "don't do that" a lot and sometimes, we're told, "I'm trying to keep you safe". Keep us safe from what?? Failing, isn't that what we are supposed to do to learn? If we were not juggling knives, how could trying something different hurt us? Were we near a bridge that we could fall off? I love "that can't be done". Why can't it be done? I tried one way and it did not work, does that mean I cannot try again another way? Think outside the box... This is the start as to how we all get to that point in time, that we no longer take chances, think outside the box and try and try again. Failing… we all do it. How do you handle the failure? Depends on how you were brought up. I always felt like a failure. But I have changed my mindset to show that failure is part of the plan, failing forward. A winner is a loser who tried one more time. ~Jim Rohn.

Learning How To...

Back to my family now that you have learned a little bit about me and my family. I will speak of them through the rest of the book and who knows what else will come out about any of them. Of course, all good!! Even when there are hard times, truths that come out that are hard to handle, but never without a hug, an "I love you" and them always standing by your side, never leaving us!

With all that happened in my life, I always had to learn how to adapt, change and move on amongst anything else that I needed to learn to do. But the biggest thing I had to learn how to do was change my mind set. If my mind set were different then, I guarantee you my life would have turned out differently. It is so easy to slip back into the old ways. It is because it is what you know, and it is familiar to you. To change, grow and learn you must get uncomfortable. This is where you learn to fail forward. Yes, you will fail but learn to fail forward. If it did not work, try something else until it does work. You might have to try several different things for it to work.

I won my court case in family court, but that did not mean a lot. My grandfather dying, was so much more important than a court case. I went through a lot with testifying. I had to learn how to relive what happened to me. I had to tell the judge and the others in the court room what happened and still hold my head high. It was rough telling my story in the court room. It is supposed to be a safe place. There is a judge to make a decision on whether you are telling the truth or not and court officers to make sure that things don't go wrong in the court room. I found out how that happens too. To be honest, it was terrifying. And that is putting it mildly. I was wishing I would die before I had to testify. But God had other plans for me. There were things I am supposed to do in this life, like live it and have a great one. But I did not know how I was supposed to do that.

I had to learn how to… do a lot of things and change myself for the better. I felt I had to do it all alone, on my own. I had my family, but they could not make my life better, that was up to me. I worked hard, to make money to get a car, afford the insurance and gas, it was all me. My mom and dad were not there helping me with payments. I always felt like working to make sure that you had a good life was not enough. Because while you were working to make your life a good one, you were working for a company that was making more money the harder you worked, and your compensation was not always equal. Do not get me wrong, there are some great companies out there, and there are bosses that do care about you and will go above and beyond to help with your life situations. I remember one boss always helped me out when I had to take my grandmother to appointments. He always worked with me and at that time, that was what I needed. I felt there was something more and there is, but you must learn how to get it. I had to learn that profits are better than wages. I learned this from Jim Rohn. He explains that wages make you a living (paying your bills) but profits make you a fortune. I knew that but had no idea how to make a profit unless I owned my own business. But I always thought you had to have one business, turns out that in order to really make it and have everything you want, you have to help many people and you can have more than one business. Multiple incomes to help you make the life you want. I am still learning which businesses work for me. One of them will be writing this book and my book signing!! I'm glad you're still reading this book and I hope to see you at my book signing. Another form of revenue will be my bookkeeping business. And yes, essential oils.

This is where I need to learn to... do all of this. That is why I am with Living Fierce Club. I was on one of the zoom calls from Living Fierce Club when I got the name of my book. Why NOT Me to have all of this? Why NOT Me to have a better life for myself and my family. Lots of "why not me". I want to have a better life and do not want to be working for someone else to make them rich. I want to be able to enjoy my life more and be with my family and show them they can have a better life than I had. Give them the mindset I am learning about now at age 48.

I have learned that there are monsters in the world. I have met them personally. I also learned that there are angels in the world too. I listen to Jim Rohn a lot. He is wonderful to listen to. If you are interested in starting to change, listen to him. The disc I listen to, Jim says we all have the same wind that blows upon us. What helps or hurts us is the setting of the sails of that wind. YUP, mindset again coming into play here and with everything. How will you handle the good and the bad, because we all encounter it! How you react is how you will have things come back to you. Another thing my grandmother taught me, what you give out comes back to you tenfold, bad, or good.

So, we must learn to decide what do we want to do in the world. Yes, what about the mean people? Do we go back at them with mean stuff? Most of us do, I am guilty of it too. Maybe not voicing our thoughts, but our thoughts are also put out there. Tenfold comes back even with thoughts, so mean people, people who think they are better than you and treat you poorly, give them good, blessing thoughts and if you can't, give it to God to do and you go about your business. Make sure you have a handle on your thoughts! Not so easy to do with the things going on in your life and the world. Everything affects you. It does not affect us all the same way.

To learn to do something different, you must try different things. I started by journaling, repeatedly. Jihan has a reset she does with the Living Fierce Club. When I enroll in them, she helps with journaling. I need to stick to it on a regular schedule, something I am horrible at. But when I did, it really helped. What I did do was write some "I am" statements. Then read them every day! I also read "Your Word Is Your Wand" by Florence Scovel Shinn. Lots of help with thoughts and then I got her other book, "The Game of Life and How To Play It". I started writing down some more of her statements. Things I wanted for myself and my family. How to ask God for help and read them every day. Your needs will change due to your situations and how things happen in your life, so you can ask for different things. It is not just all up to us to get it, it is asking God for help and allowing His miracles and blessings being given to us. Yes, God has blessings to give to all of us, and we stop them from coming. By not having faith, not letting God work in our lives. Look at the animals in the world. Yes, they go hunting and must make their homes. But all relying on God. Knowing that it will all come when needed. We must learn to pray, listen, and obey.

Life... it Happens

Ok, so life happens to everyone. There are no exceptions to this. Everyone is included!!!! Like it or not! I started writing this book in July 2020 and now it is October 2020. Yes 3 months have gone by that I have not picked up and continued writing. I tried to spend some extra time with my kids and of course working. But I can tell you that some things have not changed. I might not be on a couch in a hotel, I am home sitting in my bed, but my dog, Roxie is still by my side! I am grateful that there are no fire alarms going off.

So, one thing I talked about is mindset. I have some hard times still happening and I got into my old mindset. See, I am not perfect, and I have not mastered all the things I am working on. It is called being HUMAN! I got "comfortable" in my old mindset again. See, as much as I did not want to be there and I knew that I was there, I was unable to get out of my own head. What I should have done was enlisted the help of my people. Yes, figure out who is in your inner circle. They will always stand behind you and always have your back. When you ask them for help, they are the ones who are always there to help no matter what is going on. For me, that would be my husband, and a few select people I trust.

Since I did not enlist any help, I got into my old mindset and stayed in my "comfortable" zone. See, you need to get uncomfortable and out of the comfort zone to grow and continue to grow. The devil wants you to stay in your comfort zone, because if you do not grow, he grows bigger.

Here's just a little background of what has happened. My husband had got hurt at work, back in November 2019. His boss did not make Joe fill out any paperwork for workers' compensation. Joe went home that day and figured he would just rest his hand (he does auto body, so his hands are how he makes a living) and go back the next day, which he did. But while working, his hand hurt so bad, he had to leave. Again, his boss did not make him fill out any worker compensation paperwork. Joe's hand hurt so bad that he went to go to the doctors, because he said he hurt himself at work, they wanted him to go to a workers' compensation doctor. To be honest, we did not even think about which doctor he went to see. He just needed to be seen. Oh yes, let us remember, going to the doctors the day before Thanksgiving, it is not so easy!!! YUP I just kept praying that things would be OK with Joe. If anyone would have told me what was going to happen with Joe getting hurt, I would never have believed them!

Joe had to tell his boss to fill out the paperwork for workers' compensation so he can be seen. You only have a certain amount of time to fill out the paperwork and we were coming up on that time, 48 hours. It was crazy and we were so stressed. Not knowing what was wrong with his hand and now having to fight with his boss, it was an incredibly stressful time for the both of us. Joe finally got the paperwork and all the workers' compensation numbers to give to the workers' compensation doctors. Mindset, right, that is what this is about, well, my mindset was bad. Being human is hard!!!

Since his boss says he did not hurt his hand at work, he was fighting the workers' compensation, which means, that Joe got no workers' compensation pay, doctors are calling us for the money because they were not allowed to put it through the insurance I had. Now we had to get a lawyer and fight this in court! Now we had to deal with the court hearing and the courts shut down doing things remotely due to COVID-19. The hard time ahead of us was starting to hit me in the face. No pay meant bills were not going to get paid. Since we did not know how bad Joe's hand was hurt, we have no clue how long he would be out of work. His boss also told him to come and pick up his toolbox and get it out of the shop. I saw the writing on the wall, his boss did not want him back. Then COVID-19 hit. By the time my husband was cleared to go back to work the end of April beginning of May, his boss tells him to file for unemployment, he has no work due to the shut down of COVID-19. Yes, things kept going from bad to worse!!!

His wonderful doctor never showed up to any of her court appearances for the depositions. As much as he was able to apply for unemployment, the stress of him not working, bills piling up, my mindset was hard to keep in the positive one. There were times I was able to work on my mindset with ease and other times it was really hard to.

So, when we got back from a vacation, I wanted to spend time with my family. I was still stressed; Joe is still out of work and the court for workers' compensation case is still going on. And today, it is still going on. No ruling in the case yet. So, financially we are still struggling and trying to make things work. We did not go anywhere else and things are still not open during the summer to go do anything. I guess when you're stressed with dealing with 2020 (it is October, and it feels like we have been in this year for years already). Everyone is struggling with

COVID-19 and the effects of it. I am sure later, when talking more about COVID-19, you will hear how I feel about it, but not now. Joe has been trying to get some side jobs. He has gotten some, but not as steady as he would like. I am still working, and the kids are back to school.

Ah, school for the kids. I always got a little sad because the kids went to school, however, I also loved it because they got to learn and make friends and play. The end of last school year was horrible. By March, they were both at home trying to navigate, along with the teachers, how the hell this was going to work. The last of the third quarter just basically just review because they were expecting to go back to school soon. The world was shutting down and it was longer than anyone expected. The modifications for the new school year were all over the place and each district was different. My district, Middle Country, for high school (both my kids are in high school) so that was all that concerned us. First half of the alphabet goes into school Monday and Tuesday. The second half of the alphabet goes on Thursday and Friday. Everyone is home on Wednesday. My kids both said they wanted to go to school. Suzanne decided to change and go virtual. She had a late arrival, so since she really could not go down to the band room and was not going to see all her friends, she decided to go virtual. Keegan goes into school four days a week. Keegan is in a 15:1 due to dyslexia. A 15:1 classroom is when there are 15 kids and one teacher. The kids in the classroom are supposed to be all academically challenged, like dyslexia. This has been good for Keegan; he is getting the help and support he needs. I do not think there are even 10 kids in his core classes. Keegan is not happy about going four days a week. But his grades are better and that is a good thing for Keegan. He is in regents classes so the smaller classes and the extra help is a total win for Keegan. Although he does not think so.

Wednesday is the day Keegan struggles. No teacher around and he is not paying attention and just rushing through his work, so I have changed my schedule on

Wednesday. I get up with Keegan early and by 7am we are working on the work that is due by 1:15pm. For Keegan to get marked "present" in class, he must do his work and turn it in by 1:15pm. If the work is not done or incomplete, he gets marked "virtual absent". REALLY?!?! Yes, his IEP (Individualized Education Plan) gives him extra time… But he does not get that for Wednesday???? Yes, the things that make you go uummmmm. I could fight the school but is it worth it?

So, I had to go into my boss and tell him that I need to work from home on Wednesday or come in late. My boss picked come in late and work until 5pm. My hours are 8AM to 4PM. I do not think my boss was happy, but I know he does not want to give me a hard time. See, work has been an interesting place. There is a person in my office who has been abusive. He has been extremely abusive to me. It was brought to my bosses' attention that I have tried several times to get him to address the abuse, which got swept under the rug, a lot. You know, he has been busy running a business and does not have time to get into the office politics. It was not until someone else in the office, who knows about the abuse, went into my boss, and told him that he needs to address this or there will be problems. He finally addressed the person who is abusive to me and then informed me that it was taken care of and it should not happen again. So, the past four to five years of abuse and this person is still working there. Yes, I spoke to a lawyer and since my boss finally addressed the problem, I do not have any legal course of action right now. The lawyer also informed me that my first action, should this happen again, must be to tell my boss. If my boss does not act, I will be calling my lawyer. So, of course, my boss was not going to tell me no he was not going to work with me on Wednesdays. Just my opinion.

Ok, so now we are caught up and learning life happens, we deal with it and get back on track. Oh, yes getting back on track, I did not tell you about that! The most important thing about this book, changing for the better!!

So, I am with Living Fierce Club, which I use in conjunction with the essential oils. There is a 30-day reset that I do every time Jihan does it!! No, I have not missed one! So, I am in a reset now and it works on clean eating, movement, and mindset! Three especially important things in my life. So, doing that, I got uncomfortable, a little bit, but not enough! So, I kept going and I still pray everyday, several times a day. I asked for help to get me back on track!! Remember, I said you needed to LISTEN and OBEY!!!!! Well, I got an answer a lot sooner than I expected, or should I say, I listened and obeyed.

I saw a post from a friend I met online, through one of the essential oil groups I am in. She was looking for some people to practice on for a certification she was going for. Yup, I love being a guinea pig. Well, my call was on Tuesday at 6:30. It lasted about an hour and a half. We talked and she asked questions for what she needed to do. She is now one of my accountability people. We have never met in person, but I can tell you she is one I can count on!

No judgement with her. She is a "safe" person. She and I talked and Priya is the reason I was able to pick up the computer and start typing! We also talked about having an accountability person or persons. So, she said she would be more than happy to help me! So, guess what, I am back!!!!

Sometimes We Must Wait

In life, we want results right away. If it does not happen right away then we think, it is not meant to be. Then, sometimes, we try to make it happen because, ya know, we want it, or it is supposed to be meant to be. UM, NO!!!! I have tried to make a family relationship I lost try to work. I made sure that I tried to say the right thing, always show up for that person's family. Also just tried a bit harder with this person and his family (wife and kids). I always felt a special relationship with this family member. We are close in age and that person was always there for me when kids picked on me, always having my back and I always felt safe with this person. Unfortunately, I do not think they ever knew that. When I told about my abuse, I know that there was someone who felt responsible, BUT I never thought they were responsible at all. Never thought that way, never felt that way and never ever said it. EVER!!!! Unfortunately, I don't think this person did not feel that way.

During our talk that day, I felt my relationship with that person get severed. I still cry to this day about it. It has hurt my heart and soul so bad. I look at that person and just want to cry. It is like they cannot look at me without seeing the abuse. So, I have felt my relationship be destroyed with that person. This ultimately destroyed any relationship with my husband and my kids, I feel. Well, this was proved true recently. We had an amazing party for my cousin and her fiancée. Well, that person went to my sister, Kelly, asking if everything was OK with Suzanne. She did not say hello to that person and the family. I always make sure we all say hello and goodbye, it is extremely rude not to!! But I did not make sure the kids did this night.

See, since Suzanne was young, she always felt that this person and his family never liked or loved her. Suzanne's birthday is November 25th. It is a crazy time of year, there are a few birthdays around this time of year, along with Thanksgiving and then the holidays are in full swing!! So, getting the family together for cake and coffee was never an easy task, especially since we live 45 minutes away from everyone else in my family on the Island. I get it. Life is busy!!!

When Keegan's birthday came around in July, that person and the family would make an occasional appearance. Well, Suzanne always noticed this, never came out on her birthday, but they came out a few times for Keegan's birthday. She was never feeling the love. Was it on purpose? No, it was not. But I do feel that having to come out was much harder during November instead of July. Although, July is always busy too.

So, that person went to my sister and asked if Suzanne was OK. Well, I love Kelly!!!! She talked to him and explained that from a young age, Suzanne has always felt that she was never loved or liked by his family. He was taken a back. Do I think that they do not "love" or "like" us? NO, absolutely not, I know they love us, all of us! I think emotions are very difficult to show especially when someone hurts inside. I have reached out to him a few times about this, a while ago, so we can talk about Suzanne and how she felt. After each phone call, when I saw him, I reminded him I called him to talk to him. He said he knew, and he would call when he had a chance. That was a few years ago and he never called. I was not going to be that pain in the ass and keep calling. He knew I called, and he knew the ball was in his court. I had to let it go, I had to give it to God. I had to wait! That is one of the hardest things to do when it comes to your kids and when they hurt! So many times, I wanted to grab him and kick him or punch him, make him sit down and listen. He told Kelly that I had reached out to him, but he told her, I was scared of what Ellen was going to tell me.

There it was, right in my face. He didn't call because he had no idea if I was going to tell him if Suzanne had gone through some kind of abuse, like I had gone through.

He could not handle another person going through that. See, my abuse broke something in him.

He does not talk about his sister (my mom). His own kids had questions about their Aunt. They sat down (when they were a bit older) with their mom and dad. Asked questions about their Aunt. Well, I found out through our cousins their father got up from the table, said he will not talk about her at all, has nothing to do with her and if they wanted to know what happened they can speak to me and Kelly. My uncle did not take that talk well with his kids and wife. Which they did, which is why I know that our Uncle got up from the table and was very aggravated about the whole situation. Yes, Fran has that effect on people. Kelly, myself and our cousins went out for some pizza and we talked about what happened. They were totally shocked, and they had no idea. See, our Uncle and Aunt never spoke of her and never spoke about the abuse. Our cousins said it took their father a bit to cool down. Even over 30 years later, it still affects people, not just the person who went through it.

Kelly's conversation with him ended in him stating he was going to reach out. The party was Saturday and it's only Monday evening, so it's only been two days. I am truly hoping and praying that he does reach out. I am hoping that maybe, just maybe, in some strange crazy twisted way our relationship will start healing. It will never be what it was. Lots of years have gone by and healing from the abuse never heals 100%. There is always something there, even a scar. For him it went much deeper. I have always prayed that he found peace, but I do not know where he is with dealing with it, as he does not like to deal with it. So, healing will be hard to do. Those emotions can be very overwhelming, strong, and deep. Hell, the abuse happened to me and I know I have never healed 100% from it. I have the scars from it and I still must wake up and look in the mirror and love what I see. There are days that is easy and there are days I wish I could crawl back into bed and not get up! But I find a way to keep going. What does not kill us makes us stronger.

Changing Your Mindset

Changing your mindset is not an easy task! It is a lot of hard work and lots of fails and lots of trying again! I started by journaling. I would start with "I am" statements. Jihan taught me to write down what you want your life to be like. Write about everything!!!! When writing it down, write as if it is happening now. Do not write it like my house will have 4 bedrooms. Write it like my house has 5 bedrooms. "Will have" means you do not have it, "has" means you already have it. There is a huge difference.

Your relationships with your boyfriend, girlfriend, spouse, children, family members, and friends. What do you want your relationships to look like with these people? How you and they interact with each other. Who gives whom the surprise dinner? Or the surprise romantic night out? This list could be long! Write what each relationship will look like, as it will be different since each person is special to you in different ways.

Write down what you see your house like, every single detail, it is so important! Fireplaces, how many and where? How many rooms? What color are they painted? What does your furniture look like? Modern or country? Carpet or hardwood floors? Bathrooms, ya know you need them!!!! How many in your house?

Write about your vacations you will go on. Notice the "s" on vacations, plural, more than one!!!! Where will you go? With who? How long? What type of place will you be staying at? Resort or a Bed and Breakfast place? Family and friends around on any of them? Or just some time for you! What would you do with your time for you? Weekend spa get away?

Write about MONEY! I am debt free, is how I would start! I am debt free! See, there is an "I am" statement and how to start writing about money! Two different areas for writing, but so particularly important!! Talk about how you would give to charities that are important to you. Me, I am giving to Cystic Fibrosis. Yes, it is important to me that they get a cure for this. My daughter carries the gene for this horrible disease! She needs to be careful, if her husband has the gene for it too, there is a good probability their children will have this disease. I am horrified by it!! I will also start looking into doing something for children who are abused and/or in foster care. I have not figured out what I am going to do yet. I must look for something that the funds will be useful and helpful! Who knows, maybe this is something I am meant to start up, but I need to finish this book first! I have a lot of things on my plate but need to get some finished and off so I can continue to do my work I want to do. I give to my church which is extremely important to me and my family. They do so much good, that I feel they need to be supported and we, as a family, feel we need to do our part.

Write about things you want but as if you have them now! Not I am going to get such and such. That will not work. Mindset is everything. You are training your mind that you have it and it is yours already and the universe will get it to you. YOU must move though. You cannot sit still and wish for it. You, need to have movement. Here is a perfect example. Me writing this book and I am thinking of others to write also. HAHAHA I never thought I would even think, say, or write that, write another book. But after today, you can bet your bottom dollar I will be! See, the book is already written because I am thinking of what it is going to be already. I even might have a name…. OH, see how you get on fire and it just keeps going, the momentum. Movement do not just sit there!!

Figure it out what you want to do. Start your own business, write a book, become something, but do movement towards it! So, what if you fail?? We all fail!!!!! I have several times! Know how many times I started writing this book?? Well over twenty!!!! I even started it over two years ago too! YUP, I stopped several times. But when it came into my mind, I started again, because I had a better idea. Nope, then I had a BETTER idea! OH no!!! I stopped, but then MY BEST IDEA CAME AT SOME CRAZY HOUR IN THE MORNING! OK, we are staying with the crazy one! Um, must I remind you that I even stopped writing the best one for like over three months? OK, got it?? If not, read this paragraph a million times until you do get it! It does not matter if you stop, it matters that you pick it back up, and start where you left off or start all over again, like I did. OH, YOU FAILED FORWARD!!!!! WAY TO GO!!!!! I am so very proud of you!!!! Then, do it again if you stop! MOVEMENT!!!! It works. Guess what, I am also proud of you!!!!

Write down EVERYTHING you want, what you want to do, how you want to spend your time, how you want to spend your money as if it is already happening!!! It is happening now! Start there and never stop! You can do it, because I know you can, because I wrote this book!

Now that you have started journaling, you must also read what you wrote. Reading it as it already is will be, at first a little strange. But as things happen, you will see that it

will be mind blowing! Do not ever stop journaling and

never stop reading what you wrote.

Small Changes You Can Make

Ok, so journaling is a big thing that you can do for changing your mindset. There are so many small changes you can also do. These will be your wins, if you will, until you start thinking and dreaming bigger for your bigger wins.

See, we have the "power" if you will, to heal ourselves too. We need to listen to ourselves. Listen to our bodies. Eat less crap and processed foods and eat more fruits and veggies. Watch how your body reacts to the changes. The changes will not happen overnight, but I promise there will be changes and they will be amazing. The changes that happen are amazing to your body and your mindset.

Drink more water. I work on drinking at least a gallon of water a day. I am trying to drink more than that. We are made of water do not forget. It does our organs and skin so good. Now, at times I struggle with this. What gets me through is putting vitality essential oils in my water. The flavor is amazing, the benefits of the oils are a huge plus and it's easy to have a bottle of essential oil in your pocket book or if you're crazy like me, I have a bag of just oils I carry everywhere! Yup, I sure do.

My husband, at first, called me the "snake oil salesman". For two years, he made fun of me, called me names but always let me rub the oils on his back. Well, he said something to me one night, I asked him how his muscles were feeling? I used certain oils for supporting his muscular system. He told me was not having any of those issues anymore. I laughed at him and told him I will no longer rub the oils on his back, since he did not need them anymore and he felt they did not work. He looked horrified at me! He said ok, maybe there is something to them. He finally stopped calling me the "snake oil salesman". See my mindset, when I first used the essential oils, my mindset was I do not think they will work. But they did help my son and it was MIND BLOWEN AWAY! So, my mindset changed on the essential oils. Obviously, Joe's mindset did not change with the oils, for about two years into me using the oils. Which the next mindset I had, was let us see if this works, like test number two. So, I told myself for the next year, I would use essential oils to support our bodies' systems. I learned more about the oils, what they did, and I also learned about the supplements this company makes. I got new oils and supplements every month for the first year. Yes, I gave it a year and my husband continued to laugh and make fun of me. I told him we will see who has the last laugh. He finally stopped laughing and started asking what oils he can use for this or that. See, his mindset started changing about this company. Thankfully, he was not so surprised when I had an oil or supplement for him to use, that just came right out of my mouth when he asked. Years later, we went out for an event that had dinner. I brought along my bag of oils. He laughed and said you are going to bring them? I said yes. He shook his head saying what are you going to bring them in? I said no, I will leave them in the car, just in case we need them. He said he would not need any oils. Well, joke was on him! He asked if I had DiGize in the bag. Ya know I did!! DiGize is an essential oil to help with your digestive system. He needed it that night. He ran out to the car got it and then told me he has it in his pocket if I needed it. I shook my head at him this time and said I thought you did not need any oils tonight?

See, the everyday things we do in our everyday life can change our mindset. Mine was, let's see what one full year of using these essential oils and supplements will do. I still doubted the use of these oils. I was happy to see that I was proven wrong. They work and my mindset changed on them. Even my husband's mindset has changed, from not believing they actually work to WOW, they really do work.

Write down some affirmations. Start simple or start gigantic but write them down and read them out loud EVERYDAY!!! Keep adding to it when you want or when changes arise. You do not have to make yourself go crazy for this. Me, I choose to get a book, one I got from going to convention for the essential oils I use, and I put my affirmations in that. I read them and sometimes it is just some or certain ones I will read. Depends on what I feel like when I wake up in the morning. Was the morning great or a crazy train wreck? You can have a bunch of affirmations but maybe some of them are for when your mornings are that crazy train wreck, and you need some help with the rest of your day doing better, calmer. Find that one or those for putting out to the universe that your day will be better. I have a few affirmations I say for my husband and children every day. Yes, there are mornings I forget, but they do not have to be read in the morning only. Read them later in the day or even in the evening but read them. Get into that habit.

Habits!!!!! We talked about eating, drinking water, journaling, affirmations, mindset and using essential oils. All these things are habits. Please do not change everything all at once. Pick one or two things to do. Make sure you make the time to do those things. Just do them 15 to 20 minutes a day. Now if you decided to start using essential oils, put them on, diffuse them. That will not take you 20 minutes, once you put them on or start your diffuser, you're done. So, learn about them. Pick an oil and look it up. Learn what it can do. Use the essential oils every day, several times a day.

Another thing is to meditate. Sometimes I meditate and sometimes I just sit quietly and talk to God. I had gone to services with Dianne (my Christian concert buddy) and the Pastor Mike asked if I would pray. It was like my second time to his house (yes, he holds services in his house). I looked at Pastor Mike like a deer in headlights. Of course, stuttering, I said "God please help me". I think my next sentence was I do not know how to pray. I was so embarrassed. I felt my cheeks go bright red and all I wanted to do was to crawl under a rock!! Pastor Mike took "God please help me" and ran with it! Years later, he spoke about the first time he asked me to pray. He remembered it and said it was the perfect prayer. I looked at him and said really? He said yes, we needed it that night and tonight that is what we need again. "Pastor Mike, I still do not know how to pray", he laughed at me. He said yes you do, you talk to God. See, I always thought there was a certain way to pray. I was wrong. So, take time to talk to God. Just talk to Him about your life.

Reflecting on Life

Ok, so before I try to figure out if this is the last chapter of this book, which is about mind set and changing yourself for the better, I must take a minute and show you how things happen! I started this book in July, right after an amazing woman, Jihan helped me with a zoom call she had, which she has no clue how much she has helped me!! I am not only talking about this book, but in all areas of my life!! Maybe one day I will be fortunate enough to have her as a mentor! Ok, so mindset, Jihan is an amazing woman who is my mentor. MINDSET! Speak as if it is happening now and journal the same way.

I have been reading books to help me improve my mindset and self-help books. I read them and I feel like the people who write them are amazing people and they never falter, never trip up, and never fail. But then I remember I went to a concert with my friend Dianne. She and I love going to Christian concerts!! OMG the bands we love and to be honest, when I am not listening to Jim Rohn or someone whose speaking about improving myself, I am listening to Christian music. Dianne had asked me to go to a concert with her back in 2016 in the city. Jesus Culture, we had to stand for the whole concert as she could not get seats for us. From then on, every summer we went to a concert. Dinner before the concert too. Just Dianne, me and Christian music – YUP that was our thing, and we did not get to go this year. COVID made sure of that. Hoping the world gets back to normal, I so miss my time with Dianne and Jesus Music as we call it!!

Anyway, during the summer of 2019, Dianne and I went into New York City, Radio City Music Hall to see Mercy Me and Micah Tyler. What an amazing concert!!! During the concert, Micah spoke about his life. He has a son who is sick and deals with this disease. Listening to his story he speaks about how he has faith in God, he prays to God and asks that his son no longer suffer with this disease he has. They try all this medication, and nothing is working. He is out one day and sees a friend and they are talking, and he is telling her how his son is having a rough time. The woman then asks for Micah's hand so she can pray for his son. I remember him saying (to us the crowd but in his head when she asks for his hand), lady do you not think I have been praying?? I am on my knees every day and every night praying my son no longer has to go through this. You could see he was frustrated, mad, sad and it was one of those days that every emotion was hitting him hard. All those emotions we would be going through if it were our child. Maybe you are going through this now. Having all those emotions, for whatever reason, with every right too!!!! Well, I have kept his son in my prayers along with his whole family. It is rough to go through this.

On our way home, Dianne and I were talking about Micah's story about his son. I remember Dianne telling me, how she felt about listening to Micah speak about his son. She felt she saw Micah as a person, ya know like you and me. Not a big singer with all this money who does not struggle with everyday life situations and emotions. We see all these people we follow and see that things always work out for them. But we never see the struggles and the failures they go through. Let's face it, they do; they are people just like you and me. They have this extra money we do not have, and we struggle with that, while we see them with things always working out. So, every time we fail, which we are supposed to do because we are to learn something, we should ALWAYS TRY AGAIN!!! Why you ask? Because what if the next time it works?? Then you are the WINNER!! See, we are not made to give up. We are made to make this world a better place to be in. God gave us all the tools we need to become better people, a better tribe to make this world a better place.

See, I had to start this chapter because I lost my mindset. I got wrapped up in the horrible mindset of COVID-19 and the presidential election. It has been a total crazy time on earth right now. Mindset is what gets you by in the craziness of things. People see things differently and we must remember that. What someone sees as great another person sees as horrible. People need to remember to talk to each other. Instead I see this world turning into no one talking to each other. They talk at each other. If you do not agree with my opinion, then we cannot be family or friends!! Yes, I have seen friends who have lost family members because they do not agree, UM NO!!!! People this is totally wrong. We need a difference of opinion to work things out to learn how to compromise. We need to learn to give and take. We need to learn how to lose AND win graciously.

Mindset will help when you get into the craziness of the world. When you catch yourself getting into that toxic mindset you can catch that. When I start getting into the horrible mindset, I start changing it by thinking what I am grateful for. That is another great list to make. Things you are grateful for. I have another book just for this. It is not full yet, but I am working on it. Turns out there is something almost every day you can be grateful for. Jihan, yup there she is again, another story from her. She had something come to her that she had owed some money for a business she has. She was upset and did not think it was correct, but she paid it anyway. Put a dent in her pocketbook. As she spoke to her husband about this thing that came up, she told him, we need to show our gratitude for the things we have. She explained that her and her husband go back and forth with things that they are grateful for. So, they went back and forth with things that they are grateful for. Turns out what happened was a mistake and they had returned the money to her. Instead of getting mad and letting this ruin her day and however long it lasted, Jihan and her husband turned to gratitude mindset.

Do not choose to make the easy choice and decision, you are worth the hard decision and the fight that comes with it. I know, I am doing it now and see amazing changes that happen every day. Why not me? Why can't I have everything I want? I can, I must choose to get it. I must choose to do the work and know that I am worth it. So, if I am worth it and I can ask why not me, then you should be doing the same thing for you!!! Why not you? Aren't you worth fighting for? Aren't you worth the hard decisions, the uphill battles? Yes, they are hard times, but once you get to the top of that hill, the ride down is not so hard. By then, you have done most of the hard work. That is not to say that there will never be anymore hard times or battles, but you have been there and done it before. So, DO IT AGAIN!

I know it is never "why me" anymore! That is even harder to stay then "why not me"!! Nothing comes easy to anyone. If it does, that person does not know how to handle the hard times. It is easy to procrastinate, then to do the harder thing to sit and write my book. See, I told myself, you write a book?? Hahahahahaha that would be a huge joke!!!! The conversation that happens in my head next with myself is insane!!!!! Why is that so farfetched?? UM, YOU!!!! Yup, I got a devil on my shoulder that I hate and when he gets there, it takes my mindset away!!! "Why NOT me" turns into "why me". I am not going to let that happen so easily anymore. I am worth the time and effort I will put into myself. Who will read it?? Someone who does not think they are worth it and maybe, just maybe, God will tell them, pick up THAT book and read it!!! That reader, you, might have a lot in common or just those few things in common and maybe this book will give you the inspiration you need to say YUP!!! WHY NOT ME???? Because Why NOT You??? You are worth it!!!!!!!

So, let me hear from you when you are done reading this book!! Need help? Well, I will do what I can to help, inspire and show you how I have overcome these mountains that are really mole hills. God can do wonderful things when you let Him and do not stop Him!!! So, come on, tell me what worked for you, what did not work? Someone else might need our inspiration, what worked for you might not work for me, but it might work for someone else!!!! Be the light that God gave you! You are important!!!!!

About the Author

Ellen Scaccio is a wife, mother, entrepreneur and now an author. I always had a burning feeling that something was missing from my life, yet I had so much. I finally started exploring different things to do, jumping in headfirst of course, and I started finding different things I wanted and liked to do. Never did I think that writing would have been so satisfying and therapeutic, but it has turned out to be 100% both of those things. My wish is to anyone who reads this book, they realize their worth along with the desire to work on themselves and find out what their burning desires are and then go for them. If I can do this, then you can do whatever you desire to do. Be on the lookout, I know more is coming!